ULTIMATE
MANDALA
COLORING BOOK

This Book
Belongs To

Color Swatch

Test your color here !

Before beginning to color, please place a blank page behind each one,
to prevent bleed-trough to the next page.

www.ingramcontent.com/pod-product-compliance
Lightning Source LLC
Chambersburg PA
CBHW081446250726
48662CB00009B/2960